Anita

and

"The Goat Man"

Written by Anita W. Buice

Illustrated by Alicia Brock

ᴠᴀ

Vabella Publishing
P.O. Box 1052
Carrollton, Georgia 30112
www.vabella.com

Manufactured in the United States of America

13-digit ISBN 978-1-957479-38-5

10 9 8 7 6 5 4 3 2 1

Also by Anita W. Buice:

Anita, Look at the Beautiful Hydrangeas

Chapter One: Quiet. Then Noise.

Anita's pigtails swung as she bounced out the red door and plopped on the porch of the house in Bowdon Junction. She began her game of jacks with onesies, bouncing the small red ball and scooping up her jacks time after time. She was dressed in her favorite t-shirt and her usual red shorts.

Millie, her puppy, ran circles around the porch until she stopped to lap up cool water from her bowl. When Anita got to eightsies, she felt like a break, so she took the end of her t-shirt and wiped the sweat from her brow. The sun beamed down as she played her game, as always, with serious concentration. Jacks were important to a 7-year-old girl.

Anita's grandmother, Nanny, was in her swing beside the gorgeous flower garden. It was Nanny's treasure, her pride and joy. Anita and Millie ran in circles around her and she laughed while she sipped on the lemon-flavored sweet tea.

The day was peaceful, as most summer days were in Carroll County, Georgia in 1963. From Highway 27, Anita and Nanny heard a small rattling noise, which soon grew into a racket. The clanging was all around them. They looked around to see what in the world could be making such a noise.

Anita saw something she had never seen before. Her cowgirl boots shook. She left her jacks scattered on the front porch, opened the screen door and ran inside to her Daddy, Nanny, and her mother, Mae. Her Daddy was known as "Tebo." He and Mae were cleaning up the kitchen after lunch.

"What in blazes is going on?" he asked when he saw Anita spring through the door. She ran past him into her Mama's apron, hugging her tight. Anita said, "There's a funny looking, noisy man with lots of scary goats coming down the road." She squeezed her eyes closed and covered her ears.

"Oh my heavens," Mae sighed as her initial concern melted away and she broke into a smile. "It's only Mr. Ches, the goat man."

This did not make Anita feel any better. A name like "The Goat Man" sounded every bit as scary as the noise that he and his goats were making outside.

Chapter Two: Reunion. Then Food.

There was a loud knock on the front door and a deep, raspy voice yelled, "Anybody home?"

Anita's Daddy, Tebo opened the front door, there, indeed, stood Mr. Charles (Ches) McCartney. He was known most everywhere as "The Goat Man." Anita peeked around her Mama and saw the strange man wearing overalls and goat skins and saw that something was wrong with his arm too.

She saw a ragged, old man with a long beard looking at her. He didn't look like he had bathed in years. His wrinkled skin indicated that he had been in the sun most of his life. He looked like something out of Anita's worst nightmare. They didn't happen often, but were scary when they did. So, she fully expected her Daddy, at the very least, to protect her from the goat man by sending him away.

"Well, hello Ches, how are you doing?" her Daddy asked.

"I'm doing fine, Brother Tebo," he replied. As he talked you could see the goat man's jagged teeth. "I've got a goat with a hurt leg. I was wondering if I could stay on your back lot so I can tend to him better?"

The goat man stuck out his dirty hand for a shake and hoped to get her Daddy's permission. To Anita's surprise, her Daddy, who always wanted to stay perfectly neat and clean, shook the man's hand without hesitation.

Her Mama walked to the door and smiled, "Hello, Mr. McCartney. It's an honor to have you with us again."

Anita's heart leapt in her chest. "Again?" she thought.

Her Daddy laughed, "The last time you were around here, our daughter, Anita was about two. She obviously doesn't remember you one bit."

"Well honey, you have grown like a weed." Mr. Ches grinned at the nervous girl.

Hot from her stay in the garden, Nanny had entered the kitchen to get a cold glass of tea. She heard voices and walked into the living room and greeted Mr. Ches, "Aren't you a sight for sore eyes?"

He replied, "It's always a pleasure to see all of y'all, but especially nice to see you again, Miss Viola." Mr. Ches looked around a second or two before adding, "Honey." Nanny's face flushed.

"Well look at that she's blushing!" Anita's Mama teased.

Nanny composed herself and changed the subject, "Can y'all smell my homemade peach pie I have baking in the oven?" She gushed and looked right at Mr. Ches. "Want a piece of pie after it cools, young man?"

Mr. Ches slid his fingers through his hair and nodded, "Yes Ma'am, I'd love a piece of pie." Mr. Ches hobbled into the kitchen where he sat down at the kitchen table and waited for his treat.

Nanny stepped outside the back door and brought back a freezer of homemade vanilla ice cream that

Tebo churned by hand that morning. "Want some vanilla ice cream on your pie, too, Ches?" she asked, as if she didn't already know the answer.

"Sure would," he said. "I haven't had this kind of treatment in a real long time."

"I bet not!" Anita managed not to say out loud.

Nanny released the clamp of the churn from the top of the ice cream tub, took out the white plastic spinner, and scraped off the leftover ice cream into a bowl. She cut the juicy cobbler, placed a large serving onto a china plate, and dollopped some of the delicious ice cream onto Mr. Ches' pie.

"I don't think I've ever seen an old man so happy," Anita thought to herself as she finally managed a small smile in the goat man's direction.

"This is absolutely amazing, Viola," the goat man declared with his mouth full of pie.

Anita thought to herself, "Not real good manners either."

Her Mama, her Daddy, and Anita stood in the living room not wanting to interrupt the conversation between Nanny and Ches. "Y'all keep on standing in there and your dessert is going to get cold," Nanny giggled.

Anita was holding on to her Mama's apron as she walked into the kitchen. The smell of something sweet and gooey was just too good to pass up.

Chapter 3: The Wagon. The Goats. Then the Yucky Smell.

As they were finishing up dessert, Mr. Ches tried to confirm, "So, I really can camp in your back lot again?"

Regardless of the odor of the old man and his goats, Anita's Daddy replied, "Of course, Ches, you are always welcome here."

"Thank you, I've got to work on Cooper's left hind leg. He got in a scuffle with Jack, and Coop got himself a slit-open leg that really needs to heal."

The goat man was bent over a bit and walked a little wobbly, but he seemed to get around fine. The family walked outside and discovered an old railroad caboose that had been converted into a ramshackle covered wagon. The wagon had a top and a porch that stuck out on each side.

Ches climbed on the wagon, grabbed the reins and yelled "Go". He shook the lines of the harnesses and the goats took off. Everyone breathed a sigh of relief when the goat man got to the spot he selected and the noise stopped.

"I have twelve Billy goats pulling the wagon, and four Billy goats pushing it," the goat man explained.

The rest of the herd walked in unison with the sixteen harnessed ones. Anita counted and decided there must be around thirty goats in all.

"If the boys are called Billy goats, what are the girl's called?" she asked.

"Unfortunately, they're called Nanny goats," Viola frowned.

It took a while before Anita stopped giggling.

Anita walked around the wagon and saw pots, pans, and all kind of junk hanging on the outside. All of which explained the rattling noise. Peering inside she saw kid goats, a bed, and a pot-bellied stove. She also saw Coop, the injured goat, lying on the wagon's bed. His leg was bandaged.

"Mama, why does the goat man smell so bad?" Anita asked her mother after he was far off.

Mae sighed and said, "Sometimes I forget that I am dealing with a 7-year-old who has never seen anything quite like the goat man."

"I'm glad you waited to ask me that, because we would never want to mention this and hurt Mr. Ches' feelings. He has traveled up and down Highway 27 and all around the United States with his goats. He doesn't have a home. He considers himself a Gypsy. Those are folks that travel most all of the time. He doesn't have a place to bathe everyday like we do. When he was here last time and I offered him a bath in our house, he looked at me like I was crazy," Mae told her. In fact, she added, "I've heard him say that the only time he takes a bath is when it rains and the Good Lord washes him and his goats." The family laughed at the thought.

"Mr. Ches has told me that he has traveled to almost all fifty states," Nanny said. "He said that he hasn't been to Hawaii because he doesn't think that the goats could swim that far," Nanny laughed. "But if they did make it, he said that the goats would just eat the grass skirts off of the hula girls and cause all kinds of havoc."

Anita figured havoc must mean trouble, but also figured that the goat man and her Nanny were probably both just kidding.

Chapter Four: Camping and Cooper.

After he found the perfect camping spot, Mr. Ches got down from the wagon and went into the woods. He searched through the fallen trees for short limbs and he eventually secured several armloads of excellent wood. He stacked the limbs into a pyramid-style so that they were criss-crossing each other. He took a match out of a box and set the pile on fire. It sent up heavy smoke that trailed though the sky.

Now it was time to take care of his goats. Two of his favorite nanny goats were Cam and Betty. They stood still as the goat man took off their collars. He rubbed them down and straightened their hair as best he could. "You-ins did good work today. I bet we traveled fifteen miles in all," the goat man told his ladies. "Let's get some chow now. Y'all do some grazing in this thick green grass. It oughta taste refreshin' and mighty good," Mr. Ches said. He continued, "Let me go tend to Coop first and I'll be back to feed and milk you in just a bit."

Curiosity caused Anita to slip out of her house and wander down to the campsite. She saw the goat man climb into his wagon. Mr. Ches saw her peeking around the wagon and said, "Hello Anita come right in." A little hesitantly, she climbed up into the wagon and she saw him go straight to little Coop, "How you doing, son?" Coop was lying on his bed with his head on the pillow. The goat man gave his head a rub and Coop rose up to thank him.

Starring at Mr. Ches, Anita piped up saying, "The way your goat is acting, I don't think he is feeling well and your face looks very worried too."

Grimacing he said, "Yes I am worried. Coop's leg still looks red and swollen and it feels hot when I touch it." Bending down over Coop, he added, "You know I knew that Coop's leg was red and bad before I unwrapped it." She wonders what would happen next as she gazed at Mr. Ches as he began to work on Coop's leg.

Coop bleated mournfully, "Mmmaaaaahhhhh."

With a distressed voice, Mr. Ches lamented, "Coop your bleat sounds so pitiful. It hurts me to my core. I'll gently dab some ointment on all the red areas and hope that helps you feel better. It's a good thing that I bought some new bandages when I was in town earlier." Straining to see around Mr. Ches, Anita watched as he wrapped the bandages around Coop's leg. Sighing, Mr. Ches placed a blanket on Coop's leg. He pointed at Coop saying, "That should keep you from biting at it."

Anita remarked, "That blanket should help him a lot Mr. Ches."

"Are you out here honey," Anita's mother called.

"Yes ma'am," she answered.

"Well I was worried. It is time for you to head home young lady. It's almost supper time," her Mama replied. Anita walked slowly back through the yard to her house with her Mama beside her.

Heading out of the wagon with an empty bucket, ladle, and a bag of goat kibble, the goat man told his goats, "Now y'all are going to enjoy some supper."

He went to the back of the wagon and shooed away some of the kid goats that had stayed on the wagon. Rudy hopped down and began to chew on the grass. Abbi and Flynn maaaaaaahed as Ches told them to hop down. "Go on now," he told them. They reluctantly hopped off the wagon and onto the ground. The others joined Rudy and Chester to have their supper.

Ches softly hummed to himself as he milked Gladys. He saw she had given him half a bucket of milk. "People seem perplexed that I milk y'all so easily," he told Gladys. "It's a normal, everyday thing for me. It keeps me and my kid goats alive and healthy."

"Morgana, you're next honey pie," Mr. Ches called to his following goat. He began the same milking process. He took the ladle and pulled it from the bucket, brimming with milk. He slurped down a ladle full, and then ladled some into the baby bottles he used to feed the baby goats.

Grabbing a couple of bottles, he scooped up an armful of kid goats and cuddled them into the crook of his good arm. Balancing the bottles under his chin he fed the goats. Their bellies were round. Mr. Ches seemed pleased at this point that the most important of his duties for the day had been accomplished. He gave each goat a rub down and a massage. They bleated happily.

Mr. Ches shook out the kibble from a bag for the rest of the herd to have for their evening meal. They surged forward and ate hungrily. The stream behind the family's house would give them enough water for the day.

Chapter Five: Preaching then More Worrying.

The goat man opened a side door on the wagon and said to the goats, "Looks like we are going to have to stop by the dump soon. We're running out of our people-drawing fuel."

He pulled out an old black tire from the back of his wagon and took it over to the fire. After stoking the fire he opened a can of beans with a Bowie knife. He warmed them in a pot, and began to eat.

When Mr. Ches finished eating, he threw a black tire on top of the fire. It soon emitted a horrible smell and the black smoke billowed out for everyone around to see. The goat man knew the awful smell not only helped to attract people, but helped to keep all of the bugs away. He didn't want the people to be bothered by them. He wanted them to stay longer to hear his preachin'. "Better than any bug spray ever made," Mr. Ches assured his goats.

Back at the house, as Nanny finished cooking supper, Anita, Tebo and Mae sat down to eat. The aroma in the kitchen made their mouths water. Anita looked out the window and saw the goat man's huge cloud of black smoke rising above the back lot. She screamed, "Fire! Fire!" Her Mama and Daddy jumped up from the table to look. Nanny, not even bothering to turn from the stove said, "Oh, that's just Ches calling the people to hear him preach. You know he's got that sign on the top of the wagon that says 'Prepare to meet thy God'. He said he considered himself to be a Baptist preacher.

"He can likely sell his congregation some of his goods, too," Tebo laughed.

Soon, many cars filled with people started to show up. They were worried about the possibility of a fire. They were delighted to find the goat man. They loved to hear his traveling tales and to get their picture taken with him. The ones that had been to see him before knew it would only cost them a dollar for a visit. For an extra quarter you could even get a postcard with a picture of Jack and Coop.

Nanny walked over and raised the kitchen window. "I just love to hear that man preach, even when I can't hear nor understand a word he's saying."

Mr. Ches stood on the front porch of the wagon with his arm spread out wide. He raised his hand to the sky holding the Bible in his right hand. He began to preach. People in the crowd shouted, "Amen, Brother! and you know that's right!"

Raising his voice, he preached the gospel for twenty minutes. He calmed down, wiped his brow and made sure everyone saw him sit out his cigar box. He used it as the collection plate. Ones, fives and a ten, filled the box. Later, even one twenty. There was loads of loose change, that went into that box. This money helped Mr. Ches feed his goats and buy the few things they needed to survive.

When the goat man had finished his last sermon of the day Nanny took him some collard greens, fried okra, creamed corn, cornbread, two fried pork chops, and a glass of sweet tea with lemon. Mr. Ches, who had been preaching almost all day, thought to himself, Thank the Lord! but only said aloud, "Thank you Miss Viola. It looks mighty tasty."

Quickly wolfing his meal down, he returned the dirty dishes to Viola. Mr. Ches then wiped his mouth with his nasty hanky. Nanny rolled her eyes.

Earlier in the day, Mr. Ches stopped beside the road and picked a handful of daffodils that he handed to Miss Viola. "I appreciate the nice supper, Viola. I want you to have these beautiful flowers." His long, jagged fingernails and work worn hands wrapped around the delicate flowers. Nanny took the flowers, smiled graciously and said, "Thank you kindly, and you're most welcome."

It was time for everyone to get some sleep. Lying in bed, Anita's puppy, Millie, had her head on Anita's shoulder. They both looked out her window toward the silent screen of the drive-in movie theatre just over the horizon. Anita watched and wondered about the movie. Millie probably thought about breakfast.

Anita realized, as she was almost asleep, that she wasn't afraid of the goat man anymore. She couldn't believe that she could ever not be afraid of someone or something called the goat man, but it was true, she wasn't afraid!

Chapter Six: A Hurt Human. Then a Hurting Goat.

The next morning, everyone was sitting at the breakfast table. Anita gulped down her breakfast. She rushed everyone, pleading with them to eat faster.

"Nanny, may I please take Mr. Ches my other biscuit for his breakfast?" she begged.

Nanny replied, a little tersely, "You eat your own breakfast, young lady." Then she added, "I've already made extra for Ches." Mae and Tebo stifled a laugh.

Anita pulled on her Daddy's hand to get him to hurry. "Let me finish this last sip of coffee, honey, We'll go, if it means that much to you." She hurried outside so she could see the goat man. They all walked over to the wagon. Nanny grabbed the hot biscuits and Mama got the jam.

Everyone greeted the goat man with, "Mornin'."

He answered them back, "Mornin', may I offer y'all some homemade chicory coffee. I just finished making it."

Everyone replied, "No, thank you." Tebo exclaimed, "We just now finished with breakfast ourselves."

Nanny Viola handed the biscuits and trimmings over to Mr. Ches and he licked his lips. "Viola, you make the best homemade biscuits I've ever tasted. I've tasted me a bunch of homemade biscuits in my travels." Nanny Viola beamed with satisfaction.

The goat man's presence spread around the community like wild fire. He said, with his own sense of satisfaction and joy, "Looks like I'm going to get in some mornin' preachin' too!"

Mr. Ches finished his breakfast and wiped the back of his hand against his mouth. He quickly retrieved his Bible and watched as the cars drove in. He climbed onto the front of the wagon, and began to preach. He raised his hand and first asked God to please bless his sweet Coop who was hurtin' and needs His help.

Nanny had an idea. She knew what Coop might need. She walked back to their house and made a poultice. It was her secret recipe that she had never shared. She had made one for Anita when she had the flu. It seemed to work a miracle.

Nanny rushed back to the wagon as the day's first sermon ended. Nanny and Mr. Ches climbed into the wagon and she placed the special poultice on Coop's leg.

A man, named Mr. Pom, asked Mr. Ches about his crippled arm. Mr. Ches kept the sleeve of his missing left arm pinned to the top of his overalls to keep the sleeve from flapping.

Mr. Ches addressed the crowd, "Well, you'd think it was from one of the times when I wrestled a bear, but it wasn't. I once was a lumberjack. One day, I was chopping down a huge tree and it fell on me. Everyone thought that I was a goner. Just as they put me in my coffin, I woke up." The crowd gasped. "Trust me," the goat man continued, "I was as surprised as they were. But I'm really glad I woke up. I stayed woke up and get to live with my goats. They're so sweet. I sleep with them, too. They keep me mighty warm in the winter and they are good cuddlers, too." The crowd laughed and applauded.

After all of the town folks left, Anita heard Coop bleating loudly. She hoped it meant that he too was feeling happy. "That doesn't sound very good," Mr. Ches said.

"How can you tell it doesn't sound very good?" Anita asked.

"Well, when regular people hear the goats bleat they all hear the same thing. I have been living with these children for so long that I can tell you whether their bleats are happy or sad, and believe you me, right now, Coop's bleat is not happy."

Anita said, "Maybe we need to call my doctor, Dr. Bill. He's great."

Mr. Ches replied, "Thank you, but no. He isn't country folk like us. He's a real gentleman and besides, he treats human people, not goats. And I ain't got anything like the money it would take to pay him."

Chapter Seven: A Risky Phone Call. Help at Last. Payment.

The more Coop bleated, the sadder Anita got. Tears formed in her eyes and she couldn't stand it anymore. The more she heard the goat's distressed cries, the more she worried.

More cars pulled in the field and Mr. Ches started to preach again. While everyone was focused on his preachin', Anita slipped away to her house. When she got there she looked out the window to make sure she wasn't being missed. She went to her parent's bedroom, picked up her Mama's pink Princess telephone, and called Dr. Bill all by herself.

She cuddled Millie and stretched the phone cord from the wall. She managed to sit on the end of her Mama's bed. She slowly turned the rotary phone dial.

Dr. Bill's receptionist answered, "Dr. Bill's office, how may I help you?"

It hadn't been fifteen minutes and Anita's Dr. Bill drove up the driveway. He got out of his car and said, "Let's see this goat of yours Anita."

"Well, it's not my goat," she replied. "It's the goat man's goat, but his name is Coop and he got into a fight with his brother, Jack, and got badly hurt."

Dr. Bill followed Anita down and into the crowd with his medical bag in tow. Everyone realized what was happening and let out a collective gasp. Anita's face turned red. When she saw her Mama she began to cry.

The good doctor held up his hand and said, "Anita was very brave to do this. She did the right thing. Now show me this goat, please." Dr. Bill said. The doctor and Mr. Ches climbed into the wagon to see Coop. They looked at the goat's leg. The doctor cleaned it really well. He told the goat man that he had done a wonderful job of taking care of Coop but that his wound had gotten infected and he needed antibiotics.

Mr. Ches nodded, "I don't know how I'm ever going to be able to thank you enough, doc, much less to pay you."

"How about I get one of these nice tracts with the Bible verses inside," Dr. Bill offered.

Mr. Ches was very relieved and handed him three. "I'll even throw in a postcard of Jack and Coop."

"You know," Mr. Ches added, "I love to read Robinson Crusoe and the Bible just to try to be better at what I do. I guess you've done a lot of reading, too, to get good at what you do."

"Well, I have read many medical books to become a doctor," said Dr. Bill.   I also enjoy Robinson Crusoe and the Bible the same as you do," he added.

Dr. Bill shook the goat man's hand. He waved goodbye to everyone and he gave Anita a special squeeze and said, "Thanks for the call, kiddo. Nice goat. Real nice goat man."

Chapter Eight: True Healing. Then Good-Bye.

The next morning Anita decided to go visit the goat man all by herself. Coop was still limping, but he was getting around better.

Mr. Ches asked her, "Did you get in trouble for calling your doc?"

"No," Anita sighed. "Daddy said it was the right thing to do and that sometimes little kids know more about a person's true character than grown-ups do." My Daddy told me, "Some people who don't really know children shouldn't be so jud-uh-Judge-ju." Her voice trailed off.

"I think the word you are looking for is Judgmental. I think that your Daddy's right," added Mr. Ches.

Mr. Ches started to pack up his things, and Anita reluctantly helped.

He smiled, and his yellow teeth showed up in the sun shine. This time it didn't bother Anita at all. The goat man surprised her by getting a baby goat out of his bed and handing her a bottle of goat milk to feed her.

"What's her name?" Anita asked.

"Why, it's Anita as of now," Mr. Ches answered.

"This is amazing, I've never bottle fed a goat before and I've never had a goat named after me," she giggled. "I'll miss you, Mr. Ches," Anita said with tears in her eyes. "Will you come again, sometime?" He assured her he'd be back by stating, "You'll hear me driving up again before you can turn around 3 times."

Soon he put the baby goat in its bed and climbed in the wagon. Mr. Ches called back, "See y'all soon!"

Anita waved wildly. This time she didn't quite mind the noise as much, but the smell? That was another story.

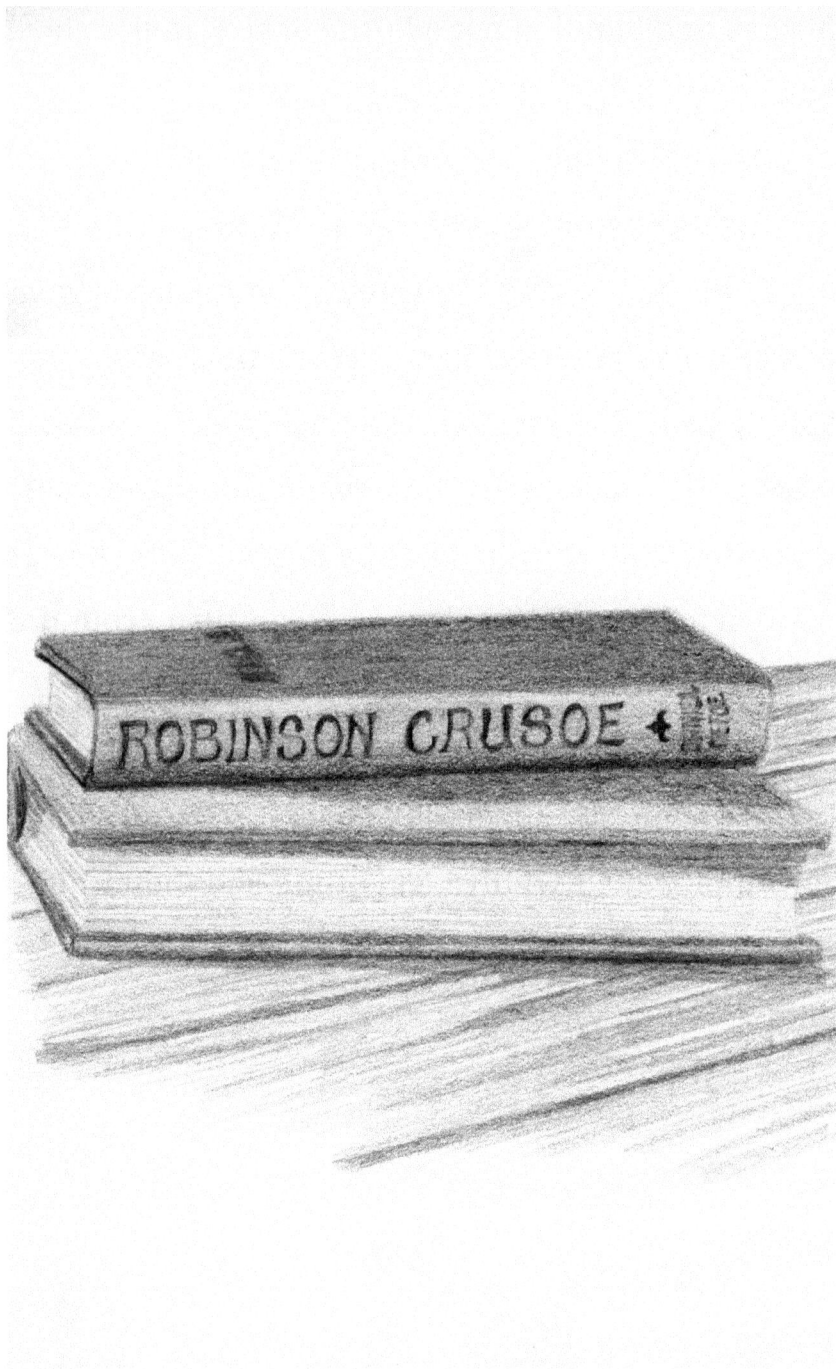

Chapter Nine: Lessons Learned.

The last couple of days had been wonderful. Multitudes of people, most of them complete strangers, had come to her back yard to see the goat man and to hear him preach and pray.

The night after the goat man left, Anita said her prayers with her Mother and Nanny. All of them bowed their heads. She prayed, "Lord, you know, Mr. Ches is very kind, even though it was very scary when he first came down the road. He's very loud and he smells and looks awful too, but I'm so glad Daddy let him stay. Amen."

Nanny then told Anita, "Mr. Ches is the perfect example of why people sometimes say you can't judge a book by its cover. Obviously, you also can't always judge a man by his looks," she smothered a laugh, "even by the way he smells."

"Anita, you were right to be careful around a stranger, her Mama added. Always be that way. But you were also right after your Daddy had introduced him to you, to give him a chance to show you how nice even such a 'strange' man can be."

"There are lots worse things a man can do with his life," her Daddy added from the next room, "than take good care of innocent animals and preach the Gospel to not-so-innocent people."

"Mama, can we visit the library tomorrow?" Anita asked. "I want to check out a copy of Robin's Son, Caruso (as the 7-year-old had understood Mr. Ches, and now quoted him). Mr. Ches told Dr. Bill that it's one of the two books he reads. I already have a Bible you and Nanny read to me. I think y'all probably need to read me that one, too."

"Yes, we sure can go to the library," Mama replied. "I don't know the Robinson Crusoe story well, but I'm sure it's a wonderful story that we can read and enjoy together." Mama turned out the light and told Anita goodnight.

Anita smiled in the dark, and thought, "One day not-so-soon I'll be a Grandmother. My meeting with the goat man is a story I'm going to tell my Grandchildren one day."

Which she just did.

The End.

Polaroid picture taken by Nanny Viola in 1963

The Goatman in 1988

Anita and "The Goat Man" is dedicated with love to Jack(son) Coop(er), Cameron, Betty and Flynn, none of whom are really goats, but all of whom are truly GOATS (The Greatest Of All Time).

Anita Buice. Author

Anita Buice grew up in the country, climbed lots of trees, and even once got her Daddy's "permission" to have a swimming pool in her Bowdon Junction, Georgia back yard "if you can dig it." Thinking he had handled that problem, her Daddy paid no attention while Anita single-handedly attempted to dig her own pool by creating a hole that took her and a sympathetic neighbor the best part of a Saturday to fill back in.

Her Daddy was more careful about his back yard thereafter, but he actually did allow The Goatman to camp there when Anita was little. Her Daddy liked The Goatman and he liked the natural fertilizer. The Goatman was a true legend and his noisy entrance into town made the preschool children hide under their desks. Anita and her family never got over his visits.

Anita loves watching musicals, basketball, and lacrosse games, and reading and listening to books. Her favorite genre is historical fiction, and it is her goal to write historical fiction for children. She lives with her adopted and mischievous kitties, Ella and Gabbi, who keep her very entertained, and she lives for her four children and the five grandchildren to whom Anita and The Goatman is dedicated.

Alicia Brock, Illustrator

Alicia Brock grew up in the great state of Georgia where she received degrees in Education, Art Education, and a Masters of Art Education. Besides working as an art and ESOL teacher in various public schools, The Helen Keller School, and as a missionary teacher in Culiacan, Sinaloa Mexico, Alicia is a working artist who has illustrated three books. She has also painted murals, and her main focus is creating bronze sculpture, pencil/mixed media, illustration, and oil portraiture, concentrating primarily on western subject matter and admired personalities known locally in her northwest Georgia hometown.

www.ingramcontent.com/pod-product-compliance
Lightning Source LLC
Chambersburg PA
CBHW061200040426

42445CB00013B/1749